effective
marriage

little
book
series

First published in 2008
Reprinted 2016
Copyright © 2008
All rights reserved. No part of this publication may be
reproduced in any form without prior permission from
the publisher.

British Library Cataloguing in Publication Data
A catalogue record for this book is available from the
British Library.

ISBN 978-1-906381-01-1

Published by Autumn House Limited, Grantham,
Lincolnshire
Printed in China

All texts are taken from the *New Living Translation* unless
indication is given to the contrary.
Other versions used include:
KJV = *King James Version*
NKJV = *New King James Version*
MGE = *The Message Bible*
NIV = *New International Version*
RSV = *Revised Standard Version*

The Bible on Marriage

'Wives and husbands ... submit to one another out of reverence for Christ. For wives, this means submit to your husbands as to the Lord. ... For husbands, this means love your wives, just as Christ loved the church. He gave up his life for her to make her holy and clean, washed by the cleansing of God's word. ... In the same way, husbands ought to love their wives as they love their own bodies. ...

'As the Scriptures say, "A man leaves his father and mother and is joined to his wife, and the two are united into one." This is a great mystery, but it is an illustration of the way Christ and the church are one. So again I say, each man must love his wife as he loves himself, and the wife must respect her husband.'
Ephesians 5:21-33

Marriage

Marriage is an exclusive union between one man and one woman, publicly acknowledged, permanently sealed, and physically consummated.

'The Bible opens and closes with a wedding.'
Selwyn Hughes

Emotional bank account

Early in marriage we learn about the emotional
bank account model of relationships. We begin to
understand that we are making either deposits or
withdrawals in the account on a daily basis.
When we are loving and kind, hundreds of credits
flow into our mate's EBA. . . .

Made in heaven?

A marriage may be made in heaven, but the maintenance must be done on Earth.

Since power struggles tear at the very fabric of relationships and leave people feeling isolated, hurt and hopeless, we'll search for a model of support that provides each partner with a balanced sense of control, enabling both partners to think of themselves as competent.

Staying committed

Talk to any couple who have been married thirty or forty years and, if they are truthful, you will hear about the bad times as well as the good. But when a couple makes it over the long haul, you'll find two strong people who have worked hard to honour the commitment made on their wedding day.

Toughing it out

Surviving all the crises of marriage over the
span of thirty, forty and fifty years plus, takes
commitment. Romantic feelings fail during the
tough times. Sex doesn't seem very important
either. Material possessions may not mean much.
Now it's the two of them against the world,
toughing it out, testing all their resources. . . .

Dry spells

Every relationship seems to have its droughts, its dry spells when growth stops and boredom sets in.

But there are two things you should not enter into prematurely: divorce and embalming.

Marriage can survive the dry spells.

Survival

What enables us to survive dry spells is the kind of commitment we make in marriage. It must allow us to experience trust, respect and intimacy. You cannot develop the openness and trust that comes with commitment in a temporary relationship when you might easily be replaced.

One hundred percent committed

All marriages are happy. It's the living together afterwards that causes all the trouble.

When both members of a couple are one hundred percent committed to each other and their commitment has been tested and has endured, uneasy fears of abandonment are significantly eased.

The most fulfilling feeling

The knowledge that you have a partner in life who is devoted to you and loves you is one of the most fulfilling feelings in life. This knowledge of an everlasting kind of love gives a deep inner security that allows you to overcome the struggles of life.

Effective communication

Highly effective marriages are the result of more than just compatibility and commitment. Effective communication and conflict management skills are vital. There will always be differences of opinion. How you handle them is what counts.

The price tag

Success comes with a price tag: time. Time spent, undivided attention given, energy expended.

'By wisdom a house is built, and by understanding it is established; by knowledge the rooms are filled with all precious and pleasant riches.'
Proverbs 24:3, 4, RSV

Commitment – a process

Commitment isn't just something that is spoken of in front of a minister. It may begin in the wedding ceremony, but commitment is a process that continues daily. It has to do with setting priorities and eliminating things that compete with your number one priority – your partner. It is observed and measured in units of time, energy, and willingness to make changes, compromise, and say, 'I'm sorry.'

'Not to worry'

When a woman gets upset, a man often tries to ease the situation by telling her 'not to worry'. He responds to her in the same way in which he relates to the situation. He doesn't recognise that his efforts to minimise the problem invalidate her feelings and make her long more and more for understanding and support.

Caring

Being cared about and understood is something
so desperately needed in this depersonalised
world that people will crawl across a thousand
miles of desert to get to it.

The sweetheart factor

Satellite dishes, big-screen TVs, and membership in country clubs do not make a woman feel cherished, but being somebody's sweetheart does.

Essential
for survival

Love is essential for the survival of all humans,
from babyhood on.

We all like to be reminded how much we're valued;
that is why God tells us how much he loves us so
many times in his book. He wants us to get the
message and not forget it!

Not a business relationship

Attentive, loving actions may be an added benefit to a man, but to a woman they are an absolute necessity. Women in a 'business arrangement' marriage are crawling their emotional walls – and their husbands aren't even aware of it.

Carry
on dating

Before marriage the three little words are 'I love you'. After marriage they are, 'Let's eat out'.

Just because you've got married does not mean that you should stop going on dates with one another.

Loved
and cherished

A woman yearns to be someone special to her husband – to feel loved and cherished. This explains why anniversaries are more important to the wife than to the husband, and why the wife feels so frustrated when her husband forgets such courtesies.

A true man

Former US president Harry Truman was an incurable romantic. He pursued his wife, Bess, for years before she finally agreed to marry him. But marriage did not end the romance. Whenever he was away from Bess, Harry wrote her love letters. After Bess Truman's death, more than 1,200 letters from Harry were found in her home. He never stopped courting his wife or letting her know she was loved, even after many years of marriage.

Emotional security

Emotional security is the ultimate goal in a woman's life. She looks for reassurance regarding her place in her husband's affections by asking him to do something for her she could easily do for herself. His willingness serves as a measure of his love.

Always number one

A man can satisfy his wife's need for emotional security by letting her know that she is the one for him – that given another opportunity he would choose her all over again.

Cherished
and valued

It is easy for a woman to begin feeling more like an object than a person. Any husband can prevent this by making her feel special, cherished and valued. Every day he needs to say something that says, 'You are important to me.'

Unconditional love

Love must be given as a gift with nothing asked in return.

A woman wants to know a man cares about her world. A man can show her he cares by becoming involved with her life.

Praise

Try praising your wife, even if at first it frightens her!

Pay her compliments. Be specific.

Compliments

Complimenting your wife will not only help you meet one of her basic emotional needs but will arouse her feelings for you. When a man does this for his wife, it will pay rich dividends. . . .

Men need compliments too!

A man needs admiration for his appearance, his abilities and his character traits.

Mark Twain wrote, *'I can live for two months on a good compliment.'*

Say it!

Don't assume your man knows how much you
admire his character traits.

He needs to hear you say it.

Ego vitamins

A wife began giving her husband five-second compliments several times a day.

She found it was as good as an ego vitamin.

Appreciation

When a man hears his wife expressing
appreciation for his support of her, it makes long,
intensive hours worthwhile. A man needs to be
appreciated for what he already is, not for what
he could become with her help.

A diet of criticism

A man wants and needs his wife's approval. A steady diet of criticism is dangerous to anyone's health. But self-esteem can be improved within an environment created by someone who values and admires their accomplishments.

'I get the point'

Few things make a man feel more loved and valued than being reassured that you grasp his point of view, even if you don't share it. Even a minimum attempt at such understanding of feelings can make an enormous difference, especially when things are not going well with a couple.

'I'm sorry'

'I'm sorry' are the toughest words to say in the English language. But say them when you need to. Admitting that you were wrong can have a powerful, positive effect on the conversation that follows.

Even if you can't see his point of view, let him know you are trying.

Women are powerful

A top-government official told his wife, 'If you ever lost faith in me I'd be finished, but as long as you believe in me I can take on the world.'

A wife needs to have faith in her husband if he is to be successful.

Reassurance

Wives, offer reassurance during the low periods. If your husband fails to get a hoped-for promotion or rise, you can still express confidence in his ability to try again or to carry on.

Strengthening
the bond

Wives should remember that every time they give
a compliment or express pride in their husbands,
they strengthen the marriage bond.

Respect

When a mother respects her husband, the children learn attitudes of respect for their father. A wife should always respect her husband's ideas and opinions, but this becomes doubly true in the presence of other family members and friends.

Scolding

When a woman acts like a mother and treats her
man like a boy, he will live down to her expectations
of incompetence. When she scolds him, does
things for him that he should do for himself, or
gives him directions on how to do something he
should know how to do, she is not respecting his
abilities as an adult.

Don't 'mother' your husband!

Nothing kills passion faster than 'mothering' your husband. It affects female desire as well. Wives who 'mother' their husbands are making a big mistake.

Anniversaries *are* important!

Many a man who misses an anniversary catches it later!

Priority one

A man must feel wanted and needed, not simply endured.

'Performance'

The media portrays men as sexually assertive and confident. But truthfully, the average male worries a great deal about his ability to 'perform'.

Affair-proof

When a wife anticipates and enjoys sex, this increases the husband's confidence regarding his masculinity as well as his ability as a lover.

Nourishment

What nourishes a marriage most?

Fancy homes? Exotic holidays? Powerful positions? Big salaries?

None of the above.

The food that nourishes a marriage is meeting emotional needs.

Don't be a talking machine

A wife giving reasons for the failure of her marriage said, 'He asked me a question and answered it himself. He told me he wanted my opinion, and then he gave me one.'

Acceptance

No quality is so vital or fundamental to a marriage
as acceptance. It is the foundation of a highly-
effective marriage. Love comes first, but acceptance
of a partner must be practised on a day-to-day
basis or love will not last.

Crisis time

After fifteen years of my nagging and complaining,
my husband asked for a state-of-the-marriage
meeting. After he had said his say, I told him that
I had learned he didn't need my suggestions for
improvement – he needed my acceptance and
encouragement. I assured him I was going to
become a new wife. And, ever since, I've been
in new-wife mode.

What *is* acceptance?

Acceptance is viewing your partner as a worthy person. That you like him/her just the way he/she is.

Should we pretend our mates are perfect?

Of course not! We must recognise imperfections but make a conscious choice to concentrate on all the good qualities, all the possibilities that lie within our partners. We accept the total person – faults and all.

The total person

When I accept my partner, I see the total person –
faults and good qualities. I am content with what
I see. And I prove my contentment by not trying to
change my partner.

A loving spouse . . .

. . . can see the good in you even when you can't.

When our need for acceptance is not met, we feel rejected, alienated and deeply hurt.

The key to acceptance

An important prerequisite to accepting a mate at face value is the ability to accept yourself as you are. To the same degree you are able to accept yourself, you'll be able to accept your partner.

The greatest barrier

There is no greater barrier to a highly-effective marriage than deep-seated feelings that you are unlovable. First you must learn to love yourself. Secondly, remember, *God* loves you. Only then will you be fully able to love another person and allow that person to love you.

Destructive habit number one: nagging

'A nagging wife is as annoying as the constant dripping on a rainy day. Trying to stop her complaints is like trying to stop the wind or hold something with greased hands.'
Proverbs 27:15, 16

Love-busters

One of the most common love-busters used by women is nagging. *But men are not exempt from the nagging habit.*

Any habit that makes your spouse unhappy threatens the love and security of your relationship.

Anger

'Let not the sun go down upon your wrath.'
Ephesians 4:26, KJV

Remember: Any time anger succeeds in marriage
it does so at the expense of love.

Destructive habit number two: angry outbursts

If you want your marriage to end, subject your partner to angry outbursts of criticism.

Destructive habit number three: criticism

'Women always marry a man and hope he'll change. Men always marry a woman and hope she'll never change.'

The changing-your-spouse process is fraught with peril!

Stack every bit of criticism between layers of praise.

Quarrelling

*'It's better to live alone in the corner of an attic
than with a quarrelsome wife in a lovely home.'*
Proverbs 21:9

If a man had enough horse-sense to treat his wife
like a thoroughbred, she wouldn't turn into a nag.

Destructive habit number four: irritating habits!

'If you are always biting and devouring one another, watch out! Beware of destroying one another.'
Galatians 5:15

Remember: he doesn't do it on purpose to annoy you. It's how he is.

A log in your eye?

'Why worry about a speck in your friend's eye when you have a log in your own? . . . How can you think of saying . . . "let me help you get rid of the speck in your eye" when you can't see past the log in your own eye? Hypocrite! First get rid of the log in your own eye; then you will see well enough to deal with the speck in your friend's eye.' Matthew 7:3-5

In any given situation, some of the fault belongs to you.

Christ, our Example

Since Christ is our Example in all things, the knowledge that we are freely accepted by him with all our imperfections should liberate us to be more accepting of others.

Think on!

Before criticising your wife's faults, you must remember it may have been those very defects which prevented her from getting a better husband than the one she married.

Cooling-off time

It is senseless and unproductive to attempt to
solve a problem when both partners are upset.
Take time to cool down and gain perspective first.

Tact

There are times when offensive behaviours, as well as mistakes, should be pointed out. You may be the only person who cares enough to do this. How do you do it?

The same way a porcupine makes love: very carefully.

The real thing

'Love one another with genuine affection, and
take delight in honouring each other.'
Romans 12:10

In the course of a marriage there are dozens of
human differences with which we must learn to
live, even if we don't like them.

Through prayer and practice, we can learn to raise
our tolerance levels and accept basic differences
by separating the deed from the doer.

Complementary

View your mate's personality differences as complementary to your own.

One of the worst mistakes you can make is to try to recreate your spouse in your own image.

Say it out loud

Acceptance is something that needs to be verbalised.

Tell your mate that you accept and like him/her just the way he/she is.

Laughter

'A merry heart doeth good like a medicine.'

'A cheerful disposition is good for your health; gloom and doom leave you bone-tired.'
Proverbs 17:22, KJV and MGE

The ability to laugh at yourself and with your partner will do more to take the edge off marital discord than anything else you can do. Laughter is a wonderful tonic when you are handling problems.

Self-healing

'Physician, heal thyself.'
Luke 4:23, KJV

Even when one partner is not willing to work on
the relationship or effect change, the other partner
can alter their own habits. Frequently the change
becomes so significant that the 'silent partner'
will join the willing partner in working on the
relationship.

Self-change

Whenever you change the manner in which you have been reacting to a situation, you change the situation.

Any situation can be changed by changing your reaction to it.

Abiding

*'Those who remain in me, and I in them, will
produce much fruit. For apart from me you can
do nothing.'*
John 15:5

The secret of self-change is in abiding in Christ.
You cannot expect to make any permanent,
positive change in your life without Christ's help.
You *can* change when you realise that your ability
to break a bad habit comes from God.

Quotes about change

'The difficulty with marriage is that we fall in love with a personality but must live with a character.'
Peter Devries

A bad habit is like a leaky roof. If it isn't repaired, it will cause more and more damage until the plaster caves in and the ceiling is destroyed.

When we change ourselves, others tend to change in response to us.

Is change possible?

'Can an Ethiopian change the colour of his skin? Can a leopard take away its spots? Neither can you start doing good, for you have always done evil.'
Jeremiah 13:23

Aside from the grace of Christ, change is impossible. With the grace of Christ, 'all things are possible'. With a word he can arrest Niagara in its fall and bid it leap back. His grace can cause the leprosy of inbred sin to cease its hold, never again to pollute the soul.

Constructive change

The very act of doing something you don't usually do seems to have a constructive impact. Constructive change in one person usually opens the way for constructive change in the other. With some people the change will come quickly, easily. Barriers built up over the years may come tumbling down.

A doormat?

Should you become a doormat? Do you have to
accept every mean, degrading, ugly, vicious thing
your mate does? Should you permit a mate to
stamp all over your rights and dignity, saying
nothing at all, to preserve the concept of
acceptance?

NO!

You are an individual, a person to be respected,
a human being with a will of your own.

You need not, for example, accept infidelity or
abuse.

Nevertheless . . .

Regrettable situations arise in which acceptance is a challenge. Nevertheless, there is nothing as beautiful as a loving relationship in which each adapts to and accepts the other as they are.

Becoming an accepting person

We all long for one person on this planet to accept and love us just the way we are – physical features, faults and all.

This should be our objective in marriage – *to be that person for our mate.*

Communication

Communication is what sparks the caring, giving, sharing, and affirming that are present in intimate friendship.

Many reasons exist for the inability to communicate. The most obvious is that most of us have never been taught effective communication skills. Another is that we are afraid to share real thoughts and feelings with our mates.

Listening

Listening sounds simple, but it is a serious and often difficult business. It involves observing non-verbal communication, eye contact, watching for underlying motives, asking the right questions, giving appropriate responses.

Listening is one of the most neglected and least understood of the communication arts.

Listening bloopers

Poor listening stems from bad habits. Two of the most irritating of these are interrupting and lack of eye contact.

Interrupters spend their time forming a reply while waiting for a split second when they can break in.

A lack of eye contact conveys lack of interest, distrust and want of caring.

Thinking
and speaking

Most of us speak at the rate of 100-150 words a
minute. Fast speakers talk at 170 words a minute
and have gusts of 200 words a minute.

But we can listen at the rate of 450-600 words a
minute. That means that we can think five times
faster than we can talk. The difference between
the two speeds is called lag-time.

That accounts for why spouses often claim never
to have heard you. What has not been heard has
been said when the listener's attention was
focused elsewhere.

Louder than words

All body responses and emotional expressions are part of non-verbal communication. Few people grasp the importance of non-verbals. In normal communication, the words used or the content accounts for only 7% of what is conveyed. Tone of voice and gestures amount to 38%, and facial expressions alone account for an astonishing 55%.

Facial expressions

Because a total of 93% of what is communicated
is done without words, understanding non-verbal
communication is probably more important than
any other listening skill.

Facial expressions are a part of body language,
and the strongest silent message sent.

Keep listening

Keep listening for feelings and continue to act as an escape valve for the airing of feelings. Sometimes it is necessary to prod gently to uncover the true emotion behind the words.

Important!

Once private feelings are exposed you must restrain the urge to give advice, criticise, blame or make judgements. This is not the time for that.

Sharing and caring. A great pattern for intimacy!

Games husbands play

The husband attempts to punish his wife by ridiculing and embarrassing her in front of their friends. He can hurt her when they are alone, but in front of friends he can really cut her down.

Control killer messages you are sending. When you do, you will notice that you and your mate draw closer to one another without conscious effort.

The silent treatment

Both men and women use the silent treatment as a weapon or form of control. To clam up, withdraw, and refuse to talk about an issue does more to clog communication than any other killer message.

Silent partner

According to marriage counsellors the 'silent husband' lies behind half of all troubled marriages.

There are reasons for male silence, and the wise woman will seek to understand her silent partner.

Little digs

Be careful how you use language.

You can send your marriage to an early grave
with a series of little digs.

High-level talks

John Powell describes five levels on which we
communicate. Level five: small talk. Level four:
factual conversation. Level three: ideas and
opinions. Level two: feelings and emotions.
Level one: deep insight.

Deep insight is the most difficult of all levels to
master. But if you fight shy of levels one and two
you will never reach the intimacy possible in your
marriage.

Wrong tone

Ninety percent of the friction of daily life is caused by the wrong tone of voice.

I-messages

Being married teaches us at least one valuable lesson – to think before we speak.

I-messages let your partner know you have negative feelings without attacking or ridiculing. You are more likely to be heard because these messages are less threatening.

'I feel hurt. . . .' That is a fact the husband can hardly argue with.

Vive la différence

Rather than assuming something is wrong with
your partner when you come up with different
conclusions, why not accept these differences as
part of God's marvellous plan for male and
female?

The speaker sex

A Harvard study indicates that women really *do* talk more than men. The average male speaks 12,500 words a day. The average female doubles that with 25,000! When a man gets home from work he has reached his word limit. His wife, however, has expended only 12,500 words. That explains why men are silent in the evenings, and women never stop talking.

Is it OK to fight?

Couples who say they never fight are deluding themselves or are entirely out of touch with their emotions. Those who refuse to acknowledge the need to fight will suffer from displaced anger such as hostility, emotional instability, depression, a long list of health problems, and a lack of intimacy.

Conflict resolution

Tips for resolving conflict include choosing the best time, staying on the subject, hearing the other person, and moving towards resolution with the readiness to apologise.

Shifting gears

When there are conflicts to be resolved both partners should have the right and privilege to state clearly and completely their views, feelings and reasons – without interruption.

Re-establish touch

After a vigorous exchange of views partners should be quick to re-establish touch. A simple touch of the hand, a warm hug, or bodies 'spooned' as you sleep can melt hostilities. The closeness of a hug goes deeper than words.

Walk-talk

If you are not in the habit of exercising regularly, you could begin walking with your mate several times a week. This way you can walk and talk at the same time, getting the physical benefits from exercise as well as benefits to your marriage.

Holy triangle

Husband, wife and God are a holy triangle. If communication breaks down between husband and wife, it affects their relationship with God. If the circuits to heaven are jammed, there will be a busy signal between the couple, too.

A person cannot be genuinely open to God and closed to his mate.

Talking

When a woman talks she is usually not seeking
advice, solutions, or answers. She is simply
exploring her feelings. When this necessary
exploration is cut off, it short-circuits the process
and she feels alienated from her mate.

Trust

A woman has to be able to trust her man implicitly to give her accurate information about what he is doing with his time and money (as well as everything else). Trust is foundational to a highly-effective marriage. Without honesty and trust there can be no openness between the couple, and every conversation will be inhibited.

What husbands can do about PMS

Learn what kind of support your wife wants during this time; it differs from woman to woman. Encourage her to walk, and walk with her. Give her a break from household chores. Whip up a healthy meal for her, or take her out to eat.

A tranquil home

A group of men were asked what they wanted most at home. Expensive furniture? Swimming pools? A BMW in the driveway?

The majority said *tranquillity.*

The dog-eat-dog atmosphere of the workplace calls for a tranquil atmosphere in the home.

Stress and
the male

Both men and women suffer stress, but men
have a higher death rate from stress. Male stress
originates in four main areas: body image; career
concerns; family concerns; and the inability to
share feelings or express emotions.

Even if a wife cannot make her husband talk
about his problems, she can understand when
he becomes distant, forgetful and unresponsive.

Who's boss?

Husband and wife are dependent on each other.
Although their responsibilities and roles differ, they
are equal in importance, and both are necessary to
the well-being of a healthy society.

Think it through

*'Wives and husbands . . . submit to one another
out of reverence for Christ. For wives, this means
submit to your husbands as to the Lord. . . .
For husbands, this means love your wives just
as Christ loved the church. He gave up his life
for her. . . .'*
Ephesians 5:21-26

Ponder especially the meaning of the words 'this
means love your wives, just as Christ loved the
church'.

Dictatorship?

Male dictatorship receives no support in Scripture. The dictator often isolates and alienates himself from his spouse as well as others in the family. His controlling nature usually kills his wife's love.

The controller's life is regulated by rules.

Because there is no mutual submission with a controller, regard for the other person or the ability to see the world from their point of view is missing. Such an approach invalidates and discourages the development of a partner's self-esteem.

Consequences of 'control'

If, in the name of leadership, a husband totally controls his wife, serious consequences may ensue. A continual suppression of her desires will eventually deaden her love for her husband, and she may attempt to get back at him in many insidious ways. She may also develop headaches, ulcers, sleeplessness, or one of many emotional cover-ups.

Spheres of responsibility

A woman needs freedom to operate within her sphere of responsibility. She needs to make decisions and changes where necessary, as well as to receive and enjoy support from her husband who encourages her in her role.

A supportive relationship

The marriage is a supportive relationship in which there is an even distribution of power and a clear division of responsibility in which each partner has a balanced sense of control.

It is a mutually submissive complementary relationship.

Models of leadership

Supportive leadership is the model for the home. An authoritarian represses individual freedom; a leader encourages freedom of thought and action. An authoritarian is uncompromising; a leader is understanding. An authoritarian is unyielding; a leader is adaptable.

A leader manages, motivates, inspires and influences in order to obtain willing co-operation.

Partnership

When a husband takes seriously the command to love his wife as Christ loved the church (Ephesians 5:25), he will establish a supportive partnership in which he never forces his wife to obey, but wisely offers tender leadership that encourages her to follow. Such supportive leadership brings harmony, happiness and God's blessing.

The control is God's

One of the tremendous advantages of putting yourself under God's control is that you have the resources of heaven at your disposal. God's Word promises that he will instruct and guide us in the way that we should go.

Don't compete – complete

God did not intend husband and wife to compete with one another but to complete one another.

'If anyone is in Christ, he [she] is a new creation; old things have passed away; behold, all things have become new.'
2 Corinthians 5:17, NKJV

The crises of life

If a man is going to lead his family effectively and survive the crises of life, he must ask the Lord to come into his life, forgive his past sins and failures, and make him into the kind of leader needed to guide his family.

To wives

'Be good wives to your husbands, responsive to
their needs. There are husbands who, indifferent
as they are to any words about God, will be
captivated by your life of holy beauty. What
matters is not your outer appearance – the
styling of your hair, the jewellery you wear, the
cut of your clothes – but your inner disposition.'
1 Peter 3:1-3, MGE

Submission

'Submit to one another.'
Ephesians 5:21, NIV

Submission is more than just something women do for their husbands. It should permeate the life of every Christian on a daily basis. Christ is our example in this process of submission.

Marriage requires endless mutual submission or give and take.

Father
and children

The most important thing the father can do
for his children is to love their mother.

Their emotional development and stability
depend on it.

Praying together

Research shows that couples who pray together are happier than couples who do not; couples who pray together frequently are more likely to rate their marriages as being highly romantic than those who pray less frequently.

Improvement

The husband will grow in self-confidence as he practises supportive leadership. The wife will notice an improvement in her attitudes towards herself and her marriage as she responds and adapts to his leadership.

Sexual desire . . .

. . . is an outgrowth of the energy derived from proper nutrition, exercise and sleep. All these affect the energy available for sexual involvement. If you want to enhance your levels of sexual desire, make sure you eat properly and get enough exercise and sleep.

Physical contact

The second law of thermodynamics notes:
'Everything left unattended will tend toward
disorder.' Living in the same house, practising
the same faith, parenting the same children,
sharing the same bed, isn't enough any more.

Four hugs a day are necessary for survival, eight
for maintenance, and twelve for growth.

A fountain
of blessing

'Let your wife be a fountain of blessing for you.
Rejoice in the wife of your youth.
She is a loving deer, a graceful doe.
Let her breasts satisfy you always.
May you always be captivated by her love.'
Proverbs 5:18, 19

No marriage is all sunshine, but two people can
share one umbrella if they huddle close.